YOU

The Golden Age of Pirates

An Interactive History Adventure

by Bob Temple

Consultant:
Sarah Knott, Director
Pirate Soul Museum
Key West, Florida

Capstone
press®

Mankato, Minnesota

You Choose Books are published by Capstone Press,
151 Good Counsel Drive, P.O. Box 669, Mankato, Minnesota 56002.
www.capstonepress.com

Library of Congress Cataloging-in-Publication Data
Temple, Bob.
    The golden age of pirates: an interactive history adventure /
by Bob Temple.
    p. cm.—(You choose books)
    Summary: "Describes the people and events of the Golden Age of Piracy.
The reader's choices reveal the historical details from the perspective of a pirate,
a navy sailor, and a merchant ship crewmember"—Provided by publisher.
    Includes bibliographical references and index.
    ISBN-13: 978-1-4296-0162-7 (hardcover)
    ISBN-10: 1-4296-0162-0 (hardcover)
    ISBN-13: 978-1-4296-1181-7 (softcover pbk.)
    ISBN-10: 1-4296-1181-2 (softcover pbk.)
1. Pirates—History—Juvenile literature. I. Title. II. Series.
G535.T45 2008
910.4'5—dc22   2007005695

Editorial Credits
Angie Kaelberer, editor; Julie Peters, designer; Scott Thoms, photo researcher

Photo Credits
Art Resource, N.Y./Réunion des Musées Nationaux, 34; Art Resource, N.Y./
Scala, 19; Art Resource, N.Y./Snark, 16–17; Corbis, 73; Corbis/Bettmann,
cover, 30; Corbis/Richard T. Nowitz, 10; Getty Images, Inc./Bridgeman Art
Library/Studio of Willem van de Velde II, 36; Getty Images Inc./Hulton
Archive/Rischgitz, 96; The Granger Collection, New York, 77; The Image
Works/Mary Evans Picture Library, 43, 51; Maps.com, 9; Mary Evans Picture
Library, 26, 55; North Wind Picture Archives, 60, 100; Peter Newark's Pictures,
12, 23, 41, 68, 81, 90, 93, 99; Rick Reeves, 6, 64, 88, 105

1 2 3 4 5 6 12 11 10 09 08 07

TABLE OF CONTENTS

ABOUT YOUR ADVENTURE

YOU are living in a time when pirates rule the world's seas. Will you fight them—or will you join them? What kind of life will your choice bring?

In this book, you'll explore how the choices people made meant the difference between life and death. The events you'll experience happened to real people.

Chapter One sets the scene. Then you choose which path to read. Follow the directions at the bottom of each page. The choices you make will change your outcome. After you finish one path, go back and read the others for new perspectives and more adventures.

YOU CHOOSE the path
you take through history.

Pirates roamed the sea,
chasing merchant ships
and their valuable cargoes.

Sail Away!

You live in a time of discovery, adventure, and travel. Thousands of men spend their lives on the high seas. Pirates roam the waters, looking for merchant ships carrying valuable cargo. Like pirates, privateers attack and steal from merchant ships. But they do it with the permission of their country. Navy ships chase pirates, trying to keep order on the vast seas. A life at sea is dirty and dangerous, full of great risks and great rewards.

Turn the page.

In the late 1400s, European explorers first traveled to the New World—now known as North America and South America. Since then, European countries have built colonies in the New World.

Merchant ships travel back to Europe loaded with gold, spices, jewels, and other treasures from the colonies. Other ships carry slaves, most of them kidnapped from Africa.

Pirates sail small, speedy ships that take them to islands and waterways other ships can't reach. Pirates look for riches to capture, and they don't care who gets in their way. Pirates are only out for one cause—their own.

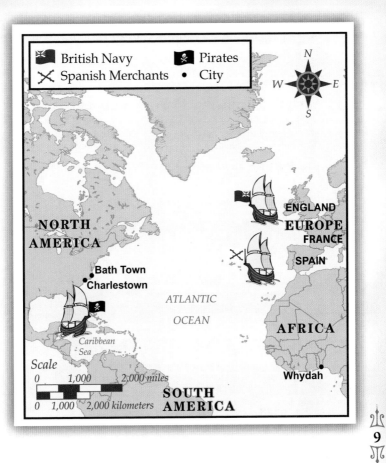

Turn the page.

You scan the horizon from the shore of your Caribbean island. You believe life at sea would be exciting. But you know about the dangers, too. Get on the crew of the wrong navy ship, and you might be treated horribly. Join a pirate or merchant crew, and every meeting with another ship could be your last.

Gold Spanish coins were just one type of treasure pirates would risk their lives to capture.

You see a ship moving toward shore. It could be a navy ship, coming to recruit new sailors. It could be a merchant ship, bringing goods. Or it could be a pirate ship, full of men with robbery on their minds.

As the ship sails closer, your excitement grows. A life at sea can be dangerous, but that's the life you've chosen. It's time to set sail.

➻ To chase pirates on a navy ship in the 1690s, turn to page **13**.

➻ To carry treasure on a merchant ship in the 1680s, turn to page **35**.

➻ To be a pirate and sail on a pirate ship in the 1710s, turn to page **65**.

Ship crews faced danger from storms and attacks at sea.

CHAPTER 2

In the Navy

The ship is flying the flag of England's Royal Navy. It has come to recruit new men into service. You know this means volunteers would be eagerly accepted. Other able-bodied young men might be forced into service too.

You thought you wanted to join the navy. But is it really a good idea? You could end up on a ship where you are mistreated—with little chance of escape.

What will you do? Will you volunteer to serve the Royal Navy, or run and hide?

➤ To volunteer to serve in the navy, turn to page **14**.

➤ To change your mind about serving in the navy, turn to page **18**.

You've heard stories about the horrible conditions on navy ships—about cruel captains who starve and beat their crewmembers. But you don't believe them. You desperately need a job. Now one is landing right at your feet.

You run toward the navy ship as it docks. As you cross the gangplank, you almost crash into a tall, muscular man standing at the rail. He grabs your arm.

"Who are you and what do you want?" he barks.

"Take me to the captain! I seek to join the Royal Navy," you answer.

A slow, sly smile spreads across the man's face as he lets go of you. "A volunteer, eh? Well, I guess you'll do. Follow me."

As the ship heads back out to sea, you quickly discover the true nature of your captain. He puts you to work at the most backbreaking jobs. You clean the ship, man the sails, and rarely sleep. And you keep your eyes on the horizon for pirate ships. This isn't the life you hoped for. Still, you remind yourself that you are serving your country.

Days turn into weeks. Weeks turn into months. Your filthy body aches from the hard work. Your belly aches from lack of food. Your captain keeps the crew in line with severe punishments.

One morning, you spot another ship on the horizon. It's difficult to tell what kind of ship it is. Your captain orders that your ship head in its direction.

Turn the page.

As you get closer, you see that the ship is a sloop. The black flag of the small, quick ship gives away its identity. It's a pirate ship! It appears a battle is at hand.

Pirates' small, quick sloops (right) easily overtook the slower navy ships.

❖ To wait to see how the other ship reacts, turn to page **20**.

❖ To attack the other ship, turn to page **21**.

You have heard stories about the horrible conditions on navy ships. Backbreaking labor, little food to eat, and beatings from cruel captains are common. You want no part of it. Seeing the ship edge closer, you know that you need to hide. If you are caught, you will be pressed into duty.

As you run away from the shore, you spot a local tavern. The bartender there is your friend. He's an older man, so he will not be forced into navy service. You hope he will help you.

You burst through the door. As your eyes adjust to the dark room, you see there are few people inside. All the young men have gone into hiding. A few older men sit at tables, drinking ale.

Public places like taverns were good spots to find men to force into navy service.

You call to the bartender. "The Royal Navy is near," you say. "Can you help a friend?"

The bartender offers you a seat at the bar. But you think hiding in the back might be a better idea.

➤ To hide in the back, turn to page 24.

➤ To sit at the bar, turn to page 32.

"Bring it about!" the captain shouts. Your captain wants the ship turned toward the sloop. You grab the riggings to adjust the sails and turn the ship.

The sloop inches closer. It is much smaller than your ship. Smaller ships are usually fast. But this ship is moving very slowly.

"She looks sick!" one of your crewmates yells. "She's listing to one side."

Something does seem to be wrong. You've heard stories about pirate ships pretending to be in trouble, only to turn and attack.

"Cap'n, it could be a trick!" you shout. Now, it's up to the captain to decide. Will your ship attack or wait?

→ To turn and attack the pirate ship, turn to page **21**.

→ To hold off on the attack, turn to page **22**.

Your captain wastes little time. "All hands on deck!" he shouts. "Attack!" He doesn't care if the pirates can hear him. He knows they were expecting a battle. Besides, the sloop is smaller and appears to have fewer crewmembers and weapons than your ship.

On your captain's order, you fire the first shot from the swivel cannons. The cannonball sails intentionally over the bow of the sloop. It's a warning shot. If the pirates surrender now, their lives will be spared.

But the pirates know this move. They've used it many times themselves. And they know that surrender means the loss of their freedom and maybe even their lives. Besides, it's not in their nature to surrender. They'll fight to the death.

Turn to page **26.**

You see some pirates at the rear of the sloop. They appear to be pulling something in. Suddenly, your captain shouts.

"It's a trick!" he screams. "They're going to attack us!"

Before your ship's crew can react, it's too late. The pirates were dragging their anchor behind the ship. Now, they pull it in. The sloop sweeps in alongside your ship. Instantly, you know you are in trouble.

Pirates swing over the rail of your ship. Others stay aboard the sloop and fire the guns. They are careful to fire toward the rear of your ship. The pirates don't want to sink your ship. They want to own it.

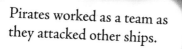

Pirates worked as a team as they attacked other ships.

Turn to page 28.

Ignoring the bartender, you rush to the tavern's back room. You squeeze into a small space between the boxes and crates. Just as you settle in, you hear a crash in the bar. The sailors are here!

"Ahoy there, mates!" one of them calls. "Any young men here who want to join the service of the Royal Navy?"

The bartender senses trouble. If the sailors can't force someone into service, they might become angry and destroy the tavern. The bartender motions toward the back room.

Quickly, they find you. Two sailors jump on you, beating you with their fists. The sailors slap shackles onto your wrists and drag you into the street. As you reach the ship, you look back at the town where you've spent your whole life. Will you ever see it again?

In your first few weeks aboard the ship, your treatment gets worse. You are regularly worked to exhaustion. When you protest, the captain gets out the cat-o'-nine-tails. The whip's nine stinging ropes tear the flesh on your back. You have never felt such pain.

Late that night, you hear quiet talk of a mutiny. Some of the crew are planning to take over the ship and throw the captain overboard. They will then sail under a pirate flag. You know that a failed mutiny could end in your death. But you can't continue to live as you are now. You wonder if deserting at the next port might be a better idea.

➤ To join the mutiny, turn to page **29**.
➤ To wait and desert, turn to page **31**.

Cannons were often used in battles between navy and pirate ships.

Right away, the pirates attack. The sloop pulls alongside your ship. Most of the pirates leap or swing on ropes onto the deck of your ship.

A bloody, hand-to-hand battle follows. Pistols, knives, and even chains are used. You fight harder than you ever thought you could. Quickly, your crew gains the upper hand.

As the number of pirates shrinks, the remaining few surrender. Your captain boards the pirate ship first. You and the other sailors follow. You search the sloop for anything of value. You're in luck—the pirates must have just loaded up with supplies. There's plenty of food and drink to keep your crew fed for weeks to come.

THE END

To follow another path, turn to page 11.
To read the conclusion, turn to page 101.

Even though they are poorly armed and outmanned, the pirates quickly gain control of your ship. Their surprise attack and fighting skills are tough to overcome.

You find yourself in hand-to-hand combat with a pirate. He slashes at you with his razor-sharp knife, wounding you. As you crumple to the ground, he jumps on your back and wraps an arm around your neck. You smell the stench of his breath against the side of your face. In an instant, it is all over.

The pirate quickly checks you for valuables. Finding none, he throws you overboard.

THE END

To follow another path, turn to page 11.
To read the conclusion, turn to page 101.

As the sun rises, so does the crew. You and 20 other men surprise the captain and his officers with knives and pistols. Several of the captain's key men are quickly defeated.

You and another crewmember burst through the door of the captain's quarters. You grab him before he can defend himself. It would be easy to kill him, but your group has other plans.

"The cap'n needs a taste of his own medicine," one man calls out. The captain remains silent as another crewman pulls out the cat-o'-nine-tails. "What's the matter, cap'n? Cat got your tongue?"

Turn the page.

Many sailors became pirates after they mutinied against cruel captains.

As the captain receives his punishment, you run a black shirt up the mast. The makeshift flag tells the world the new order of this ship.

Your days in the navy are over, but your time on the seas is not. You're a pirate now.

THE END

To follow another path, turn to page 11.
To read the conclusion, turn to page 101.

While the others plan their mutiny, you make your own plans. When the ship pulls into its next port, you will make a run for it.

As the ship comes ashore, you volunteer to help recruit new sailors. The captain agrees, but he is suspicious. He pulls the first mate aside and tells him to watch you.

In the city, you hide inside a dark building. After what seems like hours, you slip out into the alley behind the building. Free at last!

To your horror, the first mate blocks your path. "Leaving us so soon?" he asks. As he drags you back to the ship, you know what awaits you. It will be a punishment worse than any you have received before.

THE END

To follow another path, turn to page 11.
To read the conclusion, turn to page 101.

Shortly after you sit down at the bar, a man takes the seat to your right. It's clear he's a navy sailor. He reeks of months at sea.

"An ale for me and one for my friend here," he says to the bartender, motioning to you. You try to refuse the drink, but the sailor insists.

The bartender puts a tankard of ale in front of you. As you pick it up, you hear a clinking sound at the bottom of the metal mug. Instantly, you know what's happening.

You've heard of this trick before. According to English law, any man who accepts a shilling from a navy member is automatically enlisted. Sailors sneak a shilling into a man's drink. When the man pulls out the coin, he is forced to join the navy.

"I believe I've lost my thirst," you say. You slide the tankard to the unsuspecting man to your left. Slowly, he drinks the beer, then notices the coin. He smiles broadly at his discovery and dumps it into his hand.

"Welcome to the service of the Royal Navy!" the sailor shouts. He holds tightly to the man's arm as he drags him from the bar. You let out a deep sigh of relief.

THE END

To follow another path, turn to page 11.
To read the conclusion, turn to page 101.

Spanish merchant ships were
prime targets for pirates.

CHAPTER 3

Transporting Treasure

The Caribbean port city in which you live is a dangerous place. Your parents died when you were very young. Since then, you've spent time in orphanages and alone on the streets. In either case, you were fighting for food. You want to escape.

One day, you are fishing near the shore. You haven't had any luck, and your belly aches from not eating for days.

You spot a large ship sailing slowly toward the harbor. It appears to be a Spanish merchant ship. This could mean a wonderful opportunity for you.

Turn the page.

Spanish merchant ships often carry important cargo. They travel from Spain to the Spanish colonies. There, they gather the riches the Spanish government seeks—gold, silver, jewels, and spices. Those missions can be bloody, as the native people of the colonies fight against them.

Merchant ships were always on the lookout for pirate ships wanting to steal their cargoes.

But the dangers don't end there. Carrying such valuable cargo across the ocean is never easy. Pirates search for merchant ships, hoping to steal their treasure. However, the rewards are great for merchant crews that do make it back to Spain.

The ship could also be an English privateer ship. The English government wants to destroy Spain's hold on its colonies. England has given privateers permission to capture Spanish ships. They then claim the cargoes for England.

Either way, you've been waiting for this opportunity. You hope to become an apprentice on the ship. You'll learn a trade and also have regular meals and a place to sleep.

❧ *To travel on a Spanish merchant ship, turn to page **38**.*

❧ *To travel on a privateer ship, turn to page **42**.*

As the ship pulls into the harbor, you see it is a merchant ship. You offer yourself to the ship's quartermaster as an apprentice. He welcomes you aboard. Based on your age and your ability to climb, you are assigned to the ratlines. You will climb the rope ladders to adjust the masts and sails. You'll even get to stand as a lookout in the crow's nest.

Your first few days are tough. The captain works you to the point of exhaustion. You get only scraps of food. And there isn't enough space below decks for everyone to sleep. That leaves you huddled on deck, wet and shivering, as you try to sleep.

After a few weeks, you wonder about your decision. Should you have stayed on shore? Life at sea isn't any easier. Still, you've learned that your ship carries precious cargo. You try to focus on what lies ahead—incredible riches and a hero's welcome in Spain.

One morning, you're working in the crow's nest. You spot a ship on the horizon. Your heart thumps in your chest. "Ship ahoy!" you scream to the men below.

Immediately, the captain and crew spring into action. No one is sure if the ship is a friend or an enemy, but everyone must be ready. Crewmembers quickly load the cannons. The captain unlocks the weapons hold. Everyone prepares for a fight.

Turn the page.

As the ship comes closer, your captain makes a discovery. "It's the ship of Captain Henry Morgan!" he shouts.

Just hearing Morgan's name fills you with fear. Morgan is an English privateer. He has a letter of marque from the English government. This document allows him to capture other countries' ships and claim their cargoes for England. Morgan shows no mercy as he attacks merchant ships and raids Spanish coastal cities.

Your captain must quickly decide to fight or flee.

Henry Morgan was one of the most coldhearted and successful English privateers.

➤ To stay and fight Morgan's crew, turn to page **44**.

➤ To flee from Morgan's crew, turn to page **45**.

As the ship nears the harbor, you see the flag of England on its mast. Then, you see him on deck. It is Captain Henry Morgan! He is one of the most famous and feared English privateers.

Morgan never pulls into a port without a reason. He raids and captures port cities that are under Spanish rule. He ransacks the town, killing and capturing townspeople. All the while, he demands to be taken to where the city's gold, silver, and other valuables are hidden. He rarely stops until he's satisfied his thirst for treasure.

In a flash, Captain Morgan's men leap over the rails of the ship. That's when you realize that your town is next. Will you stay and fight to defend the town? Will you flee? Or will you join Morgan's forces and live a life at sea?

Pirates would stop at nothing in their search for treasure.

➤ To join Morgan's crew, turn to page **46**.

➤ To stay and fight, turn to page **48**.

➤ To run away, turn to page **50**.

The captain's decision is firm. You will stay and fight.

You have a sick feeling in the pit of your stomach as Morgan's ship closes in. You know that in the next few minutes, your life may be over.

"Help me! Oh, please, help me!"

One of your crewmates has fallen and become tangled in the lines. He hangs by one leg, screaming in pain. Left up there, he can't possibly survive the battle. You know you can climb the ratlines in an instant and help him. But a battle with Captain Morgan awaits. What will you do?

→ To stay on deck and fight, turn to page **58**.

→ To climb the ratlines to save your crewmate, turn to page **62**.

44

Morgan's reputation is too awful to ignore. Your captain issues the order to flee.

The crew quickly adjusts the rigging to turn away. You climb the ratlines to work the sails into proper position. Clinging to the ropes, you jump down, lifting a sail into position. Still, the wind isn't catching the sails. Your big ship isn't moving quickly enough.

Meanwhile, Morgan's smaller, quicker ship is headed directly for yours. It fires a cannonball over the top of your ship. It is a warning to your captain to surrender or expect a bloody battle. It's clear that your ship will not be able to escape. The crew must choose to surrender or fight.

➻ To fight, turn to page 58.

➻ To surrender to Morgan's crew, turn to page 54.

Morgan's crew is large and fierce. But they are also smart. They know that your town is not a hiding place for Spanish valuables. They have come only to restock the ship with food and other needs.

As the crew streams ashore, you step forward. One of them grabs you as the others run into town.

"I seek to join the service of the King of England," you tell the sailor. His hand loosens around your neck. He grabs your arm and marches you back to the ship.

On deck, your knees shake as you stand before Captain Morgan himself.

"He wants to enlist," the man says, throwing you to the deck.

Morgan laughs out loud. He looks at his crewman. "You know what to do," Morgan says.

Turn to page 52.

Morgan's crew numbers in the dozens or more. Quickly, you realize this fight will be mean and ugly. But you won't stand by while Morgan destroys your town.

You watch as the crew moves from building to building, house to house. They are looking for treasure, for information, and for strong young men to join their crew.

Some people are captured and brought back to the ship for information. They'll be beaten and whipped if they don't tell where the riches can be found.

Finally, a small group of Morgan's crew catches up with you. They carry large knives and pistols. You have only a small knife and lots of courage, but you will fight them.

But they see a different purpose in you. You're young and strong. They will kill you if they have to, but they'd rather have you join their crew.

There are three of them and one of you. You manage to wound one of them in the arm, but another strikes you with the blunt end of his knife. Everything goes black. As you wake up, you are being dragged back to the ship.

Turn to page 52.

Captain Morgan's reputation is well known. You have no interest in serving on his crew. And you know he will kill any man who refuses to join. You have no choice but to run.

You head into the oldest part of the city. Along the way, you call to anyone who can hear, "Captain Morgan and his men are here! Save yourselves!"

You dive into the back of a small shop. You kneel down among the boxes. Sweat streams down your face. You try to quiet your breathing, so you won't be found. Off in the distance, you hear the screams of Morgan's men. They are roaming the streets, stealing valuables and grabbing able-bodied men.

Before long, you hear them nearby. You peer out from behind the boxes and you see them—two men entering the shop.

They see you, too. They run in your direction, and you leap to run. But another man is waiting for you. You try to fight, but the three of them quickly overtake you.

In 1671, Morgan and his men captured and burned Panama City, Panama.

Turn the page.

The sailor takes you below deck and puts you in shackles. You are not sure if you are a prisoner or not. But you are sure that this ship is the smelliest, most horrible place you have ever been.

For the next few nights, you are brought up on deck. But it is only for the enjoyment of the crew. You are forced to run between two lines of sailors while they poke you with knives and sharp sticks. You run until you collapse. Then your crewmates replace your shackles and toss you below deck.

After a few days of this treatment, you are allowed above deck to work. Your body aches with every movement. But you know that stopping to rest will only make things worse. You are given very little to eat, but at least you are not being tortured any more.

One day, you hear a call from the crow's nest. There is another ship nearby. It appears to be a merchant ship. "Shall we attack, cap'n?" one sailor calls.

Morgan calls his chief crewmembers around him. You can hear them talking. They know the ship may carry Spanish riches. But right now, Morgan's crew needs food and supplies more than it needs treasure.

Morgan calls for a vote of the crew. Just like many other decisions aboard this ship, majority will rule. How will you vote?

➤ *To vote to attack the ship, turn to page 56.*

➤ *To vote to stay on course, turn to page 59.*

Morgan's boat is sleeker and faster, and he commands it well. Your captain decides to surrender. He believes that it is your crew's only chance. You help raise a white flag up the mast.

Morgan's crew eases his boat alongside yours. They quickly hop aboard your ship, ready to fight. But you and your crewmates offer no resistance.

Then you see Morgan. He boards your boat and seizes your captain. "Take me to the treasure!" he commands. Your captain slowly leads him to the precious cargo. A few of Morgan's men follow.

You hear their screams of joy when they find the riches. Morgan's men raise his flag over your ship. Then, they tie up you and your surviving crewmates. You wait for Morgan's decision on your fate.

Marooned pirates often died of hunger or thirst.

You sail for a few days until you come upon a small, deserted island. You can see from one end to the other. There are a few trees, and it appears there may be some sources of food.

Morgan spared your life, but he will leave you here. You will spend the rest of your days marooned on this tiny island with your crewmates.

THE END

To follow another path, turn to page 11.
To read the conclusion, turn to page 101.

The crew quickly votes to attack. The large ship could be carrying huge stores of gold, silver, silk, or other precious materials.

Morgan orders the crew into action. Suddenly, you are no longer being treated as a prisoner. You are an active, working member of the crew.

An officer unlocks the weapons hold and gives weapons to the crew. There are powerful guns called blunderbusses, plus knives, pistols, and swords. You nervously grip a pistol in your right hand. Two cutlass swords are strapped to your side.

Crewmembers load the ship's guns. Your speedy ship is now headed directly for the merchant ship. It looks like you'll crash. But at the last instant, Morgan orders your ship to turn. It pulls in alongside the merchant ship.

You can see the eyes of the merchant crew. They are outmanned and scared. On Morgan's order, you and your crewmates leap the rails and board the merchant ship.

A horrible, bloody battle follows. The merchant sailors are no match for your crew. Man after man, they are easily overcome.

That night, you and your crewmates celebrate the riches you've taken. Morgan orders you onto the captured ship. It is now part of Morgan's fleet, and you will sail on its crew. You'll enjoy a privateer's life for however long it may last.

THE END

To follow another path, turn to page 11.
To read the conclusion, turn to page 101.

At the last minute, Morgan's crew turns his boat alongside yours. Several of his crewmembers leap to your ship. You and your shipmates stay to protect your valuable cargo.

The battle is short. Morgan's crew kills your captain and most of your crewmates, including the man who was caught in the ropes.

Two of Morgan's crewmen throw you to the deck. They shackle you in the depths of your ship. You hear them shout as they discover the treasures onboard. Meanwhile, rats crawl near your feet, sniffing at your toes.

Your ship is now Morgan's. And you and the few other survivors of the battle will be left to die in its hold.

THE END

To follow another path, turn to page 11.
To read the conclusion, turn to page 101.

It is a close vote, but the crew decides to continue on its course. Morgan's original plan was to raid a nearby port city. He believes Spanish sailors have hidden treasure in the city's limestone caves.

Soon, you see land on the horizon. Quickly, everyone moves into position for the raid. Captain Morgan orders you to run a Spanish flag up the ship's mast. He wants to fool the townspeople. The trick works, as the townspeople continue about their business.

As the ship docks, you and the rest of the crew spill over the rails and onto the docks. You attack anyone who tries to stop you. Anyone who seems to have information is captured and beaten until they share it.

Turn the page.

Pirates sometimes used torture to get information.

You are among a group of sailors who captures a man. His clothes are ratty and torn, and he reeks of life on the open sea.

"Where are the riches from the Spanish ships?" you demand, your face just inches from his. The man shakes his head. His eyes are wide with fear.

Two of your crewmembers tie up the man and grab a whip. The more the man refuses to speak, the more you know he has information. Finally, the man talks.

Following the man's directions, the ship's quartermaster finds a cave filled with treasure. But Morgan is not done. He will continue to ransack the town until the city leaders finally pay him a huge ransom to leave. With that, your adventures at sea will continue.

THE END

To follow another path, turn to page 11.
To read the conclusion, turn to page 101.

"Hold on!" you shout to your crewmate. You put your knife between your teeth and rush to the ratline. As you reach your crewmate, you pull him upright. He clutches the rope while you untangle his leg.

Meanwhile, Morgan pulls his ship alongside yours. Morgan's men rush over the rails and jump on deck. Guns on both ships blaze, but they are useless in this hand-to-hand battle. You know what you must do—rush back down to the decks and fight.

Before you can do that, however, one of Morgan's men cuts your ratline. It goes limp in your hand and you fall down to the deck. As your crewmate falls overboard, you crash onto the deck. The impact knocks you out.

When you awake, you are aboard Morgan's ship. Ropes dig into your skin. You try to wiggle free, but the ropes hold you tight.

Morgan's men shout and cheer as they rummage through their new riches. You look around, but don't see any of your crewmates. Finally, one of Morgan's men notices that you are awake.

Just then, Morgan approaches. The crewman says, "Say hello to your new captain."

You gulp as you realize what's happened. You've survived the battle, and now you've been pressed into service as part of Morgan's crew. A whole new adventure awaits you.

THE END

To follow another path, turn to page 11.
To read the conclusion, turn to page 101.

Just like navy crews, pirates were often on the lookout for new crewmembers.

CHAPTER 4

Under a Black Flag

In your harbor town, the word is spreading. There's a pirate crew coming into port soon. The pirates are "going on the account." You know this means they are rounding up new crewmembers.

This is the opportunity you have been waiting for. Your parents died when you were a child. You were sent to live with a man who put you to work as a chimney sweep. The work is dirty and dangerous. And he feeds you barely enough to survive.

Turn the page.

You hope that a pirate crew might be willing to take you on. You're not afraid to work hard. Plus, you long for the freedom of the open sea. And you hope that great riches are in store for you. You've heard stories about the treasure that pirates capture.

You've also heard stories about the dangers on pirate ships, though. There will be fierce battles. You could end up under a captain who cares about his men, or one who is as heartless with his men as he is in battle. Still, the call of the pirate life overcomes your worries.

The ship approaching the shore is closer now. It is flying a black flag. You know what that usually means—it's a pirate ship.

As the ship comes closer, you make out the details of the flag. It shows the skeleton of a devil holding a spear. The spear points at a red, bleeding heart.

Right away, you know who the ship's captain is. Blackbeard! He is known for his violent nature. Many people think he's crazy. His crew is the most ruthless on the sea.

On Blackbeard's crew, you will have the chance to gain riches. But you may also be horribly mistreated. Do you want to sail with Blackbeard or wait for another ship?

→ To volunteer for Blackbeard's crew, turn to page **69**.

→ To wait for another pirate ship, turn to page **74**.

Blackbeard was among the most famous and feared pirates of all time.

The chance to sail with the famous Blackbeard is too great to pass up. As you step aboard the *Queen Anne's Revenge*, you see him. You realize that even the wild stories don't do him justice. Blackbeard stands more than 6 feet tall. His long black beard is twisted into braids. Some lie across his chest. Others shoot out in odd directions. Two are even tucked behind his ears.

He's a loud, boastful man. As you sail away, he shares stories of bloody battles and the great treasure he has captured.

"I tied small pieces of rope into my braids before the battle," he bellows. "As the battle neared, I lit them ablaze! With a cloud of smoke around my head, the enemy thought I was the devil himself!"

Turn the page.

As land disappears from sight, you realize that this ship is not Blackbeard's only holding. You meet other ships, all flying the devil-and-heart flag.

The fleet sails toward North America. You meet other ships along the way. Blackbeard invites pirate crews to join his fleet. If they refuse, their ships are either burned or claimed for the fleet. Merchant crews that give up their cargoes can join the fleet or sail away on their empty ships. Those that fight are destroyed.

But Blackbeard's behavior is odd, even with his crew. One night, he grabs you and several other men.

"Let's see if there are any real men on this crew," he mutters as he pushes you and the others into the deepest hole in the ship. As he climbs in after you, he slams the hatch shut.

In the hole, Blackbeard lights several smoke pots. Quickly, the hole fills with thick gray smoke. Your eyes begin to burn and water. "Please, captain, let us out!" you gasp.

After listening to several minutes of pleading, Blackbeard opens up the hatch. You and the rest of the men scramble to the deck, coughing and gasping for air. But Blackbeard stays down there for several more minutes. As he finally leaves the hole, he boasts, "I'm a better man than all of you put together!"

Turn the page.

One day, you spot the ship *Revenge*. It appears to want to flee, but when you raise the pirate flag, it slows. Blackbeard sails *Queen Anne's Revenge* alongside *Revenge*. He boards it to meet the captain.

Revenge's captain is an odd-looking man. While his ship sails under a pirate flag, he is a short, stocky man who wears a powdered wig. He looks more like a politician than a pirate. Blackbeard invites him to join the fleet, and he accepts.

You learn that the man's name is Stede Bonnet. Blackbeard wants some of his crew to serve on Bonnet's ship. What will you do?

Stede Bonnet was a wealthy plantation owner before turning to piracy.

❧ To stay with Blackbeard, turn to page **76**.

❧ To sail on Bonnet's ship, turn to page **79**.

After weeks of waiting, you hear that another ship is on the horizon. You rush to the harbor and see the black flag flapping on the mast. On the flag, the figures of a man and a skeleton raise a glass in a toast. You know what it means. It is the flag of pirate Bartholomew Roberts, the famous "Black Bart."

Even among pirates, Roberts stands out. He dresses well, often wearing bright red from head to foot. He doesn't drink alcohol or gamble. On Sundays, he holds church services aboard ship. He is known for his fair treatment of his crew and even of the crews he captures.

Still, Roberts is a pirate, and a very successful one. People say that he has captured more than 400 ships.

You are excited as you join Roberts' crew on *Good Fortune*. You can't wait for the adventures you will find at sea. Roberts prefers to sail near the coast of northern Africa, so the ship heads in that direction.

About halfway through your journey, you come upon another ship. It is carrying African slaves to the New World.

Like most pirates, Roberts has a code of conduct on his ship. All crewmembers have an equal vote. So he calls for a vote: capture the ship, or continue on to Africa?

➤ *To vote to capture the ship, turn to page* **90**.

➤ *To vote to continue on to Africa,*
turn to page **96**.

You sail with Blackbeard's fleet up the coast of North America. You feel fine, but many of the crewmembers are sick. When the ship arrives in Charlestown, South Carolina, you learn Blackbeard plans to blockade the harbor to get medicine for the crew. The city depends on ships that bring food and other supplies. Blackbeard won't allow ships in or out of Charlestown until he gets the medicine.

Blackbeard spreads out his fleet off the coast. Any ship trying to get in or out is captured. You and the other pirates strip the ships of their cargoes. You take any wealthy passengers as hostages.

The plan works. After three days, the governor sends the medicine to the *Queen Anne's Revenge*. The crew celebrates over the riches captured from the ships. When the treasure is divided, you all will be rich.

In the 1700s, Charlestown was a busy harbor town. Today, the city is called Charleston.

The fleet leaves Charlestown and heads north. In the North Carolina colony, Blackbeard visits his friend, Governor Charles Eden. Eden offers Blackbeard a pardon. He won't be tried for his crimes, and he'll get to keep his riches. But he'll have to leave the pirate life behind.

Turn the page.

Blackbeard talks over the offer with his most trusted crewmates. They decide to accept the pardon, divide up the treasure, and retire.

But you wonder if Blackbeard's intentions are as good as they seem. Will he really retire from piracy? Will all of you get a share of the treasure?

Blackbeard holds a meeting with Stede Bonnet. He is going to release Bonnet's crew, so they can also retire as wealthy men. Once again, you are faced with the choice: go with Bonnet or stay with Blackbeard.

➺ *To sail with Bonnet, turn to page* **82**.

➺ *To stay with Blackbeard, turn to page* **84**.

On Bonnet's boat, you learn that the crew isn't happy. Bonnet is not a skilled sailor or a great leader. Many of his crew are pleased they have run into Blackbeard. They believe their chances are better as part of Blackbeard's fleet.

You sail with the fleet up the eastern coast of North America. Many of the pirates on Blackbeard's ship are sick. Blackbeard knows the city of Charlestown, South Carolina, will have medicine. He is going to blockade the city, which depends on ships to bring food and other supplies. Blackbeard won't allow any ships to enter or leave the harbor until he gets the medicine.

Blackbeard's ships fan out over the harbor. As a ship tries to pass through, your ship and another one block its course.

Turn the page.

You and the other pirates then board the ship and steal its cargo. You take any wealthy passengers as hostages.

Blackbeard sends word to the governor. Unless a chest of medicine is delivered to his ship, he'll begin killing the hostages, one by one. If he receives the medicine, the hostages will be released.

The governor holds out for three days, and then sends the medicine to Blackbeard. True to his word, Blackbeard releases the hostages. The fleet continues sailing up the coast toward North Carolina.

In North Carolina, Blackbeard visits his friend, Governor Charles Eden. Eden offers Blackbeard and his crew a pardon for their crimes if they promise to lead honest lives.

Bonnet meets with Blackbeard. When Bonnet returns, he tells you that Blackbeard is releasing Bonnet's crew. Bonnet plans to accept the pardon and retire. You can choose to stay with Bonnet or rejoin Blackbeard.

Blackbeard used his fleet of ships to force South Carolina's governor to give him medicine.

→ *To continue sailing with Bonnet, turn to page 82.*

→ *To rejoin Blackbeard, turn to page 84.*

You believe Bonnet to be the more honest man. He might not be the leader that Blackbeard is, but you believe you will be safer with him. Once you have your share of the treasure, you'll return to an honest life on land.

But Blackbeard has a different plan. He and his men strip Bonnet's ship, *Revenge*, of its supplies. They remove all of the food and anything else of value they can find. All that is left is a hollow ship. You aren't sure if you should feel lucky that Blackbeard has allowed you to survive, or angry that you are left with nothing.

Blackbeard's fleet sails away. Bonnet orders that the crew head toward Bath Town, North Carolina. You sail along empty-handed. You wonder if you would have been better off staying with the crazy Blackbeard.

As you sail, you come across a group of men marooned on a small island. It is not much more than a sandbar. Bonnet recognizes them immediately—they are some of Blackbeard's crew.

You pick them up and promise to return them to land. You learn that Blackbeard played a trick on his crew so that only a few shared in the treasure.

Turn to page **92**.

Even though Bonnet seems much less cruel than Blackbeard, you've worked long and hard for a chance of treasure. You believe sailing with Blackbeard is the only way to get your fair share.

Blackbeard does allow Bonnet to sail away. But first, you and the rest of his crew strip Bonnet's ship, *Revenge*, of all its supplies. Bonnet and his crew are left with no food and no share of the treasure. The fleet sails off without them.

You believe your fate will be better. Blackbeard seems to count you among his most trusted men. He has asked you to secretly transfer much of the fleet's treasure to one ship, *Adventure*. You work with a small crew to do this. You tell no one.

But you wonder if Blackbeard is up to something. Is he going to try to sail off with the treasure? Or is he still planning to share it equally? You begin to think he has an evil plan in store. What will you do?

→ *If you think Blackbeard has an evil plan,*
turn to page **86**.

→ *If you decide to trust Blackbeard,*
turn to page **94**.

You decide that Blackbeard is planning to strand most of his crew. You are worried you might be among those left behind. You share your worries with a few crewmembers.

Unfortunately, Blackbeard learns about what you've done. He now considers you a traitor. And you know what he does to traitors.

You are terrified that he will torture or kill you, but his plan is simpler than that. The crazed pirate orders his flagship anchored. His key men round up you and several other pirates. They bind your hands behind your backs and force you into a smaller boat. A few of Blackbeard's men row away with you. You see no land, except for a small sandbar.

The men row the boat onto the sandbar. One of them pulls out a gun. "Get out," he orders. As the men row back to Blackbeard's ship, you and the other men work to untie each other.

As you look around, all you see is sand. You have no food, no drinkable water, and no weapons. You watch as Blackbeard's fleet sails off into the sunset. You know he is leaving you to slowly starve under the blazing sun.

Soon, though, you see a ship on the horizon. As it moves closer, you realize it is Stede Bonnet's ship, *Revenge*.

Turn the page.

Rescue by another ship was the only hope of survival for marooned pirates.

"Help us! We're marooned!" you and the other men scream. You jump up and down, waving your arms. The ship comes closer and closer, until it reaches the sandbar.

"Ahoy, men!" Bonnet calls. "Climb aboard!"

Just when things looked hopeless, you are saved.

Turn to page **92.**

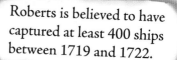

Roberts is believed to have captured at least 400 ships between 1719 and 1722.

The crew votes to capture the ship. *Good Fortune* changes course toward its target. You and the other pirates grab weapons and get ready for battle.

As your ship approaches, the captain of the other ship hails Roberts. He wants to talk, not fight.

The *Good Fortune* pulls alongside the slave ship. You and several other pirates hop over the deck rail to board it. Roberts is close behind. The captain agrees to pay a ransom to Roberts.

"I submit to your demands," the captain calls to Roberts. "Deal with me as you must. I only ask that my crew be spared."

To your surprise, Roberts allows the ship to carry on with its cargo of slaves. Roberts returns to your ship with the ransom.

"Captain, why did you let them go?" you dare ask him.

Roberts replies, "That captain showed he was a true sailor and man of character, so I allowed him to continue."

Turn to page **96**.

Bonnet sails the crew back to land. "The governor has issued a pardon," Bonnet explains. "We are all free men. We may not have riches to share, but we can all start new lives."

You all accept the pardon. You will not be tried for piracy as long as you promise to lead an honest life.

Some men will return to the sea. It is the only life they know. It is the only way they believe they will ever become rich. To them, the chance of reward is worth the risk.

Your sailing days are over, though. Your experiences with Blackbeard and Bonnet have shown you that an honest life on land might be a better way to live.

Blackbeard didn't enjoy his freedom for long. In 1718, he died during a battle with the navy.

THE END

To follow another path, turn to page 11.
To read the conclusion, turn to page 101.

As the fleet sails along, you are aboard *Adventure*. Suddenly, you see *Queen Anne's Revenge* is in trouble. It has run aground. This is surprising, because Blackbeard himself is guiding that ship. He rarely makes mistakes.

Blackbeard signals the *Adventure* to help. You and your crewmates guide *Adventure* next to *Queen Anne's Revenge*.

Another pirate leaves *Adventure* to help free the stuck ship. He works for a long time to try to free it, but without any luck. *Queen Anne's Revenge* appears to be sinking. Its crewmembers dive into the water to save themselves.

Suddenly, Blackbeard appears on the deck of the *Adventure*. You are shocked to see him. You thought he was among those who were still in the water.

Soon, it becomes clear. Blackbeard ran *Queen Anne's Revenge* aground on purpose, so he could slip away. After all, you earlier moved most of the treasure to *Adventure*.

Now, *Adventure* sails away, leaving most of Blackbeard's crew behind. He will now only have to share the treasure with 40 men, not 300 or more. But you are among the lucky. You will get a share of the treasure, and you will be able to retire without being tried for piracy.

THE END

To follow another path, turn to page 11.
To read the conclusion, turn to page 101.

Africans were kidnapped and taken to the New World, where they were sold into slavery.

Your ship continues to the African coast. Upon arriving in the port city of Whydah, Roberts' plan becomes clear. There are several slave ships in the harbor, and Roberts plans to capture them all.

Roberts barks out commands to his men. They are to move into the harbor, board all the ships, and demand a ransom. He tells the crew he has no plans to take slaves. He will allow the ships to stay afloat in exchange for the ransom.

Roberts leads the crew into the harbor. You all board ship after ship. Most of the ships are already packed with people who will be sold into slavery. The captains of these ships don't want to fight. They want to sail to the New World to sell their valuable cargo.

Turn the page.

You board one of the ships. As instructed, you seize the captain. "In the name of Black Bart Roberts, we will allow you to pass upon payment of the ransom," you say. Shaking with fear, the captain agrees.

You take the ransom and return to Roberts' ship. Most of the others do the same, and the ships sail off to sea. But one captain refuses.

"Captain, what should we do with the ship that won't pay?" you ask Roberts.

Roberts stands at the railing, staring at the ship. He turns to you. "Burn it," he replies.

You and the other pirates gulp, but you do as ordered. You know that if you refuse, Roberts' revenge will be swift and punishing.

Crews who resisted the pirates' demands were in for a fierce fight.

THE END

To follow another path, turn to page 11.
To read the conclusion, turn to page 101.

Some sailors fled their
ships for a life of piracy.

CHAPTER 5

The Power of Pirates

Piracy was widespread from about 1690 to 1725. These years are known as the Golden Age of Piracy.

During this time, England, Spain, France, and other European countries battled for control of lands in the New World.

As European ships sailed back to Europe loaded with riches from the New World, they made an attractive target for pirates. Piracy was centered on the eastern coast of North America, throughout the Caribbean, and all the way to the northern coast of Africa.

People turned to piracy for a variety of reasons. They were seeking better lives, trying to escape navy service, or hoping to become rich. Some were captured and forced into service as pirates. Others mutinied against their cruel captains and took over the ships for themselves. For them, the freedom to live as they pleased was worth the risk of punishment or death.

Most pirates' lives were anything but glamorous. Nearly all of them lasted only a few months or years before dying in battle or being executed for their crimes. Only a few managed to get out of the business and live the rest of their days in peace.

By the mid-1720s, piracy was becoming less common. Better conditions on navy and merchant ships meant that fewer sailors chose to become pirates. They could satisfy their love of the seas in an honorable way.

Also, the North American colonies—which would soon become the United States of America—began building and arming their own navy ships. This led to more attacks on pirate ships.

Countries that had tolerated piracy because it was good for business began to pass laws against it. They also passed laws that gave ordinary citizens more rights and provided better treatment for the poor. Life for most people was no longer a day-to-day fight for survival. By the 1820s, widespread piracy only existed in a few areas, such as the China Sea.

But while the Golden Age of Piracy may have ended, piracy still exists. Huge cargo ships are difficult to attack at sea, but smaller yachts and ships are still good targets for today's pirates. Their appearance and tactics may be different, but their mission is still the same—to steal on the high seas.

Pirates dreamed of bags full of coins and chests full of jewels.

Time Line

1492—European explorer Christopher Columbus sails to the Caribbean islands and claims them for Spain. Spain begins building colonies in the New World.

1600s—England, France, and the Netherlands establish colonies in the New World. The European countries fight over control of the colonies. Many of these battles take place at sea. To get crews for their ships, countries often force young men to serve in the navy.

1662—The English government issues a letter of marque to Captain Henry Morgan. He begins capturing Spanish ships and raiding Spanish colonial cities.

1668—Morgan captures the city of Porto Bello, Panama. The city pays him a ransom of 100,000 pesos to leave.

1671—Morgan attacks and burns the city of Panama City, Panama.

1688—Morgan dies of natural causes.

1716—Edward "Blackbeard" Teach commands his first pirate ship.

1717—Stede Bonnet leaves his sugar plantation in Barbados to become a pirate. Later that year, he joins forces with Blackbeard.

1717—Governor Woodes Rogers of the Bahamas offers pirates a pardon from King George I of England if they give up piracy. Enough pirates accept the pardon to cause a sharp decrease in piracy in the Caribbean.

June 1718—North Carolina Governor Charles Eden pardons Blackbeard and Stede Bonnet. In spite of the pardon, both men continue to act as pirates.

November 22, 1718—Blackbeard is killed during a battle with a navy ship near Ocracoke Island, North Carolina.

December 10, 1718—Stede Bonnet is hanged for piracy in Charlestown, South Carolina.

1719—Slave ship crewmember Bartholomew "Black Bart" Roberts turns to piracy after the captain of his ship is killed.

1719–1722—Roberts captures about 400 ships on the North American coast and in the Caribbean.

February 10, 1722—Roberts is killed during a battle with an English navy ship.

OTHER PATHS TO EXPLORE

In this book, you've seen how the events surrounding the Golden Age of Pirates look different from three points of view.

Perspectives on history are as varied as the people who lived it. You can explore other paths on your own to learn more about what happened. Seeing history from many points of view is an important part of understanding it.

Here are some ideas for other Golden Age of Pirates points of view to explore:

♦ During this time, women had even fewer options in life than men did. A few women did turn to piracy. What was life like for female pirates?

♦ Government officials had two choices: to go after pirates or to try to work with them. What was that like for them?

♦ Pirates spent some of their time and money celebrating in coastal towns. What was life like for the people who lived in these towns?

READ MORE

Harward, Barnaby. *The Best Book of Pirates.* New York: Kingfisher, 2002.

Lassieur, Allison. *The History of Pirates: From Privateers to Outlaws.* The Real World of Pirates. Mankato, Minn.: Capstone Press, 2007.

Lock, Deborah. *Pirate.* DK Eye Wonder. New York: DK, 2005.

Steele, Philip. *The World of Pirates.* Boston: Kingfisher, 2004.

INTERNET SITES

FactHound offers a safe, fun way to find Internet sites related to this book. All of the sites on FactHound have been researched by our staff.

Here's how:
1. Visit *www.facthound.com*
2. Choose your grade level.
3. Type in this book ID **142901620** for age-appropriate sites. You may also browse subjects by clicking on letters, or by clicking on pictures and words.
4. Click on the **Fetch It** button.

FactHound will fetch the best sites for you!

Glossary

apprentice (uh-PREN-tiss)—someone who learns a trade or craft by working with a skilled person

desert (di-ZURT)—to leave military service without permission

letter of marque (LET-ur UHV MARK)—a legal document allowing a ship's captain to claim the cargoes of enemy ships

maroon (muh-ROON)—to leave someone on a deserted island

merchant (MUR-chuhnt)—a person who buys and sells goods for profit

mutiny (MYOOT-uh-nee)—a revolt against the captain of a ship

privateer (prye-vuh-TEER)—a person who owns a ship licensed to attack and steal from other ships

ransom (RAN-suhm)—money that is demanded before someone or something will be set free

ratlines (RAT-lyns)—ropes tied to form a ship's ladder; ratlines allow sailors to adjust tall sails or climb into the crow's nest.

shackles (SHAK-uhlz)—a pair of metal rings locked around the wrists or ankles of a prisoner

BIBLIOGRAPHY

Konstam, Angus. *The History of Pirates*. Guilford, Conn.: Lyons Press, 1999.

Rediker, Marcus Buford. *Villains of All Nations: Atlantic Pirates in the Golden Age*. Boston: Beacon Press, 2004.

Selinger, Gail & W. Thomas Smith Jr. *The Complete Idiot's Guide to Pirates*. Indianapolis: Alpha, 2006.

Stephens, John Richard, ed. *Captured by Pirates: 22 Firsthand Accounts of Murder and Mayhem on the High Seas*. Cambria Pines by the Sea, Calif.: Fern Canyon Press, 1996.

Zarin, Cynthia. "Green Dreams: A Mystery of Rare Shipwrecked Emeralds." The New Yorker, November 21, 2005: 76–83.

INDEX

112